ABUNDANCE NOW

60 WAYS TO EXPERIENCE TRUE ABUNDANCE

ST. MARTIN'S
ESSENTIALS
NEW YORK

JESSE SANDS

First published in the United States by St. Martin's Essentials, an imprint of
St. Martin's Publishing Group

www.stmartins.com

Design by Jonathan Bennett

Library of Congress Cataloging-in-Publication Data

Names: Sands, Jesse, author.
Title: Abundance now : 60 ways to experience true abundance / Jesse Sands.
Description: First edition. | New York : St. Martin's Essentials, [2020] |
    Series: The now series
Identifiers: LCCN 2020024207 | ISBN 9781250765529 (trade paperback) |
    ISBN 9781250765536 (ebook)
Subjects: LCSH: Self-realization. | Satisfaction. | Wealth.
Classification: LCC BF637.S4 S264 2020 | DDC 178—dc23
LC record available at https://lccn.loc.gov/2020024207

Our books may be purchased in bulk for promotional, educational, or business
use. Please contact your local bookseller or the Macmillan Corporate and
Premium Sales Department at 1-800-221-7945, extension 5442, or by email at
MacmillanSpecialMarkets@macmillan.com.

First Edition: 2020

10   9   8   7   6   5   4   3   2   1

Create the highest, grandest vision possible for your life, because you become what you believe.

—OPRAH WINFREY

ABUNDANCE NOW

INTRODUCTION

There was a time in my life when I felt the opposite of abundant. I was tens of thousands of dollars in debt, and my meager paycheck barely paid for all the monthly bills that I had amassed. In fact, I often borrowed money from one credit card to pay the monthly payment for one of my other cards. If you'd asked me how I felt, I would have told you I felt like there was an enormous, crushing weight on my shoulders all the time.

And if you'd asked me about abundance, I would have told you that abundance was for other people. I wasn't born into a wealthy family, I didn't know wealthy people, and I didn't have parents who modeled financially healthy decisions. My parents were always in deep debt, and I ended up just like them. Abundance? I had no concept of what that even meant.

If you'd asked me what I wanted most, I would have told you that I wanted a million dollars, to pay off all my debt, to buy a house (instead of renting a tiny studio apartment), to finally get a car, to be able to help my parents financially, and to donate to some charities. That's as specific as I would have been. How much money did I actually need to become debt-free? I didn't actually know, because I hated looking at my bills.

Long story short, life got harder and harder. Eventually I just couldn't do it anymore. I was thinking of declaring bankruptcy, like some of my relatives had done. However, I had seen firsthand that though bankruptcy seemed like a short-term good solution, the long-term effects created different difficulties. What to do?

I started reading books on abundance and prosperity. The ideas in those books made sense. They often focused on changing at-titudes and beliefs about money. Some of them also had specific tips on what to do with money. I began to implement those ideas, and that's when things began to change.

One of the most surprising ideas I encountered is that abundance isn't solely about money. What?! I was so focused on my (lack of) wealth that I couldn't fathom abundance in any form besides money. But I kept reading and learn-ing and taking positive steps. And things be-gan to change. Some things changed quickly, and some changed more slowly, but change *was* happening. As things started to improve,

I began to realize that the books were right: abundance was a concept, not a thing. And I didn't have to wait for abundance to come my way before I could begin feeling abundant. Not to sound too woo-woo, but abundance began internally, as a mind-set, long before I could see the external results.

Those ideas changed my life, and I'm excited to share them with you here.

This book isn't meant to solve all of your abundance issues. But it can be a bright light on the path to experiencing more richness in life. Read each idea, and try each of the practices.

Do so with an open and curious attitude. Don't tell everyone you know that you're doing it, especially people who can tend to be negative. Just take time every day to read a little bit of this book, and then put the ideas into practice as best you can.

One thing to consider: Every journey has moments of success, and a few stumbles as well. If you hit a roadblock or a new challenge, don't lose heart. Double down on these ideas, and keep moving forward. Those who persevere are rewarded for their efforts. If you do something halfheartedly, you will receive halfhearted results. But if you move forward with

enthusiasm and commitment, you'll have results that match.

Your journey of abundance is your own. You
are 100 percent responsible for your own life
and your own experience. It is my sincere
hope that this book can be one of many positive forces that will help bring you greater
abundance in your life.

THE ABUNDANCE MANIFESTO

I now accept that I am worthy to experience abundance in every area of my life. I look beyond the limitations and see only opportunities. I choose to make decisions that help me to be rich in health, rich in love, rich in finances, and rich in joy. I know that abundance isn't just receiving what I want, it's joyfully giving to others. My only obstacles are the ones that I settle for, so right now I increase my ability for abundance and prosperity in my life. I give myself permission to pursue what brings me joy, making my passions more and more a priority in my life. I live a deeply meaningful life, which makes me abundant indeed.

I am unlimited in my wealth.
All areas of my life are
abundant and fulfilling.

—LOUISE HAY

WHAT ABUNDANCE MEANS

The word "abundance" makes most people think of financial abundance, an abundance of money. What do you think of when you think of abundance? Whatever meaning comes to mind, can you think of several other definitions as well?

In truth, abundance is anything that expands your life, and lack of abundance is where you feel constricted. Breathe now, and know that the more you believe you deserve abundance, the more abundance you will experience.

Try This—Journal

For many years, I've kept what I call a "Prosperity Journal." This is a journal where I record all of the different ways that I experience abundance on a daily basis. It is a constant reminder that I am always surrounded by abundance, if I only take the time to see it.

START WITH A GOAL

Every book on prosperity seems to start the same way, which is to create a goal. Knowing what you want in life makes it much more likely you'll get it. But if asked about their goals in life, most people wouldn't be able to tell you what they want with any specificity.

If you want financial abundance, how much? If you want an abundance of peace, what does that look like? If you want abundant love, how would that manifest? Having a goal doesn't mean that you will get exactly what you want, but it does mean that now you have a direction to move toward.

Try This—Goals

What do you want? Specifically? If you want money, how much? And in what forms (stocks, cash, real estate, etc.)? If you want love, what kind? More friends? A significant other? Better relationships with family? How about health? Where in your body specifically do you want to have better health? We are more apt to get what we want when we know exactly what it is we're working toward.

THE MANY FORMS OF ABUNDANCE

You can have an abundance of just about anything: money, health, love, joy, peace, energy, friends . . . even an abundance of ideas. When I was younger and had a lot of debt, I thought of abundance only in terms of having more money.

Paradoxically, while I didn't have a lot of money, I did have an abundance of fear. To turn it around, I began to pay more attention to what I had than to what I didn't have. It was a long process, but it worked.

Try This—The Variety of Abundance

Money is the most obvious way of experiencing abundance, but how many other ways can you think of to experience it?

Ultimately, it's not the money that gives you abundance, it's the feeling that money creates. And you can have that feeling anytime you want.

DOING WHAT YOU LOVE

The popular saying tells us, "Do what you love and the money will follow." What that saying doesn't mention is that sometimes it takes a while before that money will come, and you might have to work at a job you *don't* love to pay the bills before your passion can support you.

A more accurate saying might be: Do what you love and the money will follow—but be prepared to hustle at a different job in case that money is following a little *too* slowly. Trust and believe, and it *will* follow.

Try This—Abundance Partner

You don't have to walk through life alone. Pick someone to become your Abundance Ally (or Prosperity Partner, or whatever you want to call the person).

Meet together consistently, perhaps for lunch once a week, or once a month, or whatever works for you both, and discuss how your journeys to abundance are going. Help each other, encourage each other, believe in each other. You will stay more focused on bringing abundance into your life if you have a friend with you.

10 QUICK WAYS TO BE MORE ABUNDANT

Set goals for every area of your life.

Smile.

Make positive decisions
with your finances.

Think of five things you are grateful for,
right now.

Take one action immediately to change
something you don't like in your life.

Do something each day that
brings you joy.

Start each day by remembering
   that you are worthy of having
   abundance.

Travel light—forgive yourself and
   others; let negativity go.

Focus on what you have,
   not what you lack.

Find three ways to give to others
   each day.

ABUNDANCE OF LOVE

The greatest riches are found in having an abundance of love. You can have all the "things" you want, all the money you could ever want in the bank, but without loved ones, it doesn't mean as much.

I know this firsthand. When I didn't have much financial abundance, my family and friends gave me their love and help. When I turned it around and became an abundant person, I was able to share my abundance with them. That meant far more than the money itself.

Many people who order their lives rightly in all other ways are kept in poverty by their lack of gratitude.

—WALLACE D. WATTLES

Try This—Gratitude

Have you heard of a Gratitude List? This is a list you write each morning, right after you wake up, of five or ten (or any number you choose) things that you are grateful for.

Why bother doing this? As the saying goes, "Life rewards a grateful heart." If you are constantly focused on the good things in life, you tend to see more good in life, and therefore you tend to receive more good. You feel better, you enjoy your life more, and you are a positive influence on others.

ABUNDANCE, PROSPERITY, MORE

What are some other names for abundance? You can call it prosperity, plenty, luxury, richness, wealth, opulence, fruitfulness . . . and the list goes on.

Why is this important? Having a vocabulary filled with words that mean "more" allows you to expand your awareness of the many ways that you can be—and feel—abundant in every area of your life.

When you are grateful,
fear disappears and
abundance appears.

—TONY ROBBINS

EVERY FAILURE HAS A SEED
OF OPPORTUNITY

Shortly after I began my path toward abundance, I experienced a severe setback. At the time, I felt devastated, thinking that maybe my journey was just a lie and that my attempts at change had failed. But, though it was easier said than done, I decided to stay positive, and soon enough I was experiencing a new sense of freedom.

Looking back, I can see that what I thought was failure was actually an opening for a new journey that led me to new heights. Now, when something I initially perceive as negative happens, I try to see the good as fast as possible, which can help me turn the situation around.

Try This—The Abundance Question

Think of a challenge you have in your life. Now think about how you are reacting to that challenge. Next, ask yourself this question: If I truly believed in the possibility of abundance, how would I respond to this challenge?

If the answer to this question is different from the way you react when met with a challenge or setback, ask yourself why, and then choose the best way to move forward.

SAYING NO MEANS SAYING YES

One simple (but not necessarily easy!) way to bring a feeling of abundance into your life is to stop saying yes to doing things that don't bring you joy. Every time you say no to something, you are actually saying yes to yourself.

Imagine how abundant you will feel if you are able to say no to the people and the activities that drain you, and as a result are able to spend more of your time with the people and activities that bring you joy.

Try This—Less Is More

There is a famous saying that goes, "Nature abhors a vacuum." Once there is a void, life rushes in to fill it.

You can create a vacuum in your life by cleaning out drawers and closets, then giving away your old clothes and other items to verified charities. Not only will you be creating more order in your life, you will also be creating a vacuum that life will rush in to fill.

ANYTHING THAT BRINGS
YOU JOY IS ABUNDANCE

The simple secret of abundance is to choose
to see abundance wherever you are. If you
approach life with the perspective that there
is something for you everywhere, in all things,
you will truly be abundant.

Every spiritual master has taught us that,
though it's sometimes well hidden, there is

something positive in every person and every experience . . . And it's our challenge to find it. If we make that our priority, we'll see abundance everywhere we look.

Try This—Who Are the People in Your Life That Make You Rich?

Which people in your life make you feel like a million dollars? Who sees the best in you, and is always there to help? And who are the people that tend to be negative, make you feel "less than," and leave you feeling drained?

Here's a simple and obvious tip: spend more time with the people who make you feel good, and less with those who don't. The more positive people there are around you, the more abundant you will feel.

Wealth consists not in having
great possessions, but in
having few wants.

—EPICTETUS

WHAT DO YOU WANT ABUNDANCE FOR ANYWAY?

I asked a friend what kind of abundance she wanted. "I want to be a millionaire," she replied quickly. That is something that many people say. I pressed further, and asked her what she wanted the million dollars for, specifically.

"I don't know . . . ," she honestly replied. From there we had a great conversation about what she really wanted, and how much money it would require. When we finished, we knew how much she wanted, and what it was for. What do you want your abundance for?

Try This—What Would You Do If You Could?

If money were no object, what would you do with your life? What career would you have? What hobbies would you have? Who would you give assistance to, and how? Where would you travel? How would you dress? How would you carry yourself?

Write down all of the answers in your journal. Begin making each of those things come true now, without waiting for more money. Experience the feeling of abundance through the pursuit of each of those things.

AN ABUNDANCE OF HEALTH

On the L.A. Freeway one day, I noticed that the car in front of me had a bumper sticker that read, "You don't have anything if you don't have your health."

I have no idea what motivated that person to put that sticker on their Honda, but it got me thinking. I'd always heard that saying as a cliché . . . but in the end, it couldn't be more true. Without health, nothing else in your life matters. Nothing.

Giving thanks for
abundance is greater than
the abundance itself.

—RUMI

Try This—What Health Decisions Can You Make to FEEL Better?

Health is more valuable than gold. What one simple, small thing can you do today that will have a small, positive effect on your life? Drink more water? Walk or move more? Stop smoking? What else?

Choose one, and do it today. That one decision to invest in your health could yield amazing results.

MAKING PROSPEROUS DECISIONS

We sometimes think that abundance comes to us, but the truth is that abundance is a choice we make every day, all day long.

Think about it—each and every day, we have a dialogue inside our head.

We say things like "Damn, I'll never be able to afford that," or "Why am I always so broke," or

"Another bill—grrrr." How many more times a day do you focus on what you lack rather than on how much you have?

The key to abundance is
meeting limited circumstances
with unlimited thoughts.

—MARIANNE WILLIAMSON

Try This—Remind Yourself

We are often surrounded by negative images, difficult people, and challenging situations. We need to remind ourselves of the best that life has to offer. The more we remind ourselves of life's abundance, the more abundance our lives will have.

I put Post-its around the house with positive sayings (like those found in this book!). I put them on the bathroom mirror, the refrigerator, the front door—everywhere I look frequently. They remind me that throughout the course of each day we have many choices . . . and that I can choose abundance.

5 ABUNDANT DECISIONS

Right now, I accept all the abundance that flows into my life.

I choose to be a magnet for more of what I want in my life.

I am grateful for everything I already have in my life.

I refuse to see limitations; I see opportunities, everywhere.

I say yes to what brings me joy, and no to what drains me of energy.

ALIGNING EVERYTHING
FOR YOUR BENEFIT

Here's a peek into one of my daily practices. When I wake up in the morning, I remind myself what my goals are, and then remind myself that the only person who can tell me I'm worthy of them is myself.

Then I try to live up to these goals each day. If you are waiting for others to say you deserve abundance, stop. Let's check that box, now. You deserve abundance. You do. Really.

Try This—Don't Debt Any Further

This is the most basic advice I can give if you are experiencing financial debt—don't debt any further. It's obvious when I say it, and I don't say it glibly because I've been there: the first step in getting out of debt is to not debt any further.

For me, that meant cutting up my credit cards and not using them anymore. It was extremely difficult. But in the end, it was short-term pain for long-term positive results. My debt kept going down each month, and that led to a sense of momentum that eventually allowed me to get out of debt completely. If you want to get out of debt, stop debting!

Try This—A Prescription for Abundance

Take a moment and answer the following question (after taking a few deep breaths). Thinking of your life, and the goals of abundance that you have, ask yourself: "What three things can I do today that will help bring me more abundance in my life?"

Then see what actions come to mind. It can be finishing a project, reaching out to someone who could be helpful, making a call, creating a business plan, finding a Prosperity Partner, organizing your bills, or anything else that you can do immediately that will help align yourself with abundance. And then go do them. Repeat tomorrow.

MONEY, MONEY, MONEY—HOW MUCH IS ENOUGH?

How much is enough? There are many examples in the media of people who make millions of dollars and spend the rest of their lives trying to build that into tens of millions and then into hundreds of millions and finally into billions of dollars.

And yet 99 percent of the people on the planet

have very little. How much is enough? We each have to answer that question for ourselves, with great honesty.

Try This—Pay Yourself First

A wise friend of mine once told me that I should "pay myself first" out of every paycheck I received. I argued that I couldn't do that, because I had so much debt.

He replied, "Even if it's just five bucks a check, put it in a savings account. Do that before paying any bill." So I started with two dollars per check, and eventually ten dollars per check, and then more. It felt amazing to have a savings account, and to realize that I was as worthy to receive money as the people and organizations I was paying each month.

Pay yourself first, no matter how little the amount may be, and most especially if you feel you can't afford it.

GIVING IS RECEIVING

I first started volunteering somewhat reluctantly, at the request of a friend, but when I did I found out something unexpected: I loved it. I discovered that I never felt more abundant in my life than when I was giving to others. What I received from giving to others was far beyond what I gave.

Try This—Volunteer Your Talent and Time

Giving is the best way to feel abundant. One friend said his life turned around once he began giving one hour a week, each Saturday morning, to a charity. He delivered meals to housebound seniors, he picked up garbage on the side of a highway, he mentored kids who needed help, and more.

He said that that one hour, which began as a "responsibility," ended up becoming the most important hour in his life. He now volunteers several hours every week, and he would be the first to tell you it makes him feel like a millionaire.

Most great people have achieved their greatest success just one step beyond their greatest failure.

—NAPOLEON HILL

FREEDOM IS TRUE ABUNDANCE

For many years, I felt beholden to the opinions and expectations of others. My parents expected certain things from me, my oldest friends had preconceptions of who they thought I should be, and even I had expectations of myself based on an old self-image.

I didn't feel free. When I started to ask myself not just who I thought I was, but who I wanted to be, I finally began to free myself from those expectations and opinions. And that freedom is the truest abundance. I could never have expected it, but it is worth everything.

Try This—Bloom Where You Are Planted

One of my favorite books, *The Science of Getting Rich*, says (and I paraphrase) that if we wish to experience change in our lives, we shouldn't wait for a change of conditions before we act.

Rather, we should act now, and that will create the change we want to see. This means that wherever you are, and whatever the conditions of your life, you can begin to make positive actions and decisions today. Do this daily, and see what happens!

NOTHING BAD ABOUT IT

Finish this sentence: Money is the root of all . . . If you are like most people, you would answer "evil." How about these questions: What is the color of money? And the color of jealousy? Both answers are "green."

Money has a lot of negative connotations. Sometimes our beliefs—conscious or subconscious—about money actually sabotage us from accepting, receiving, or striving for more.

Try This—Everything Money Can Buy

Many people want to be "rich," or to "be a millionaire," but what do you actually want that kind of abundance for?

Make a list of all the "things" that money can buy, that you believe will make you happy. Now you know why you want more abundance, and knowing the "why" will motivate you to keep moving toward what you want.

YOU CAN'T TAKE IT WITH YOU

Big houses are cool. Private jets seem amazing. A bank account with many zeros feels safe. Lots of possessions show others you've made it. A big job title signals how far you've come.

But in the end, when you take your last breath, are those the things that truly represent abundance to you? They may be what the world looks at, but in your heart of hearts, is that what ultimately matters? For me, abundance is about the love I give, to myself and to others.

Try This—Give Today

Here's an abundance challenge for you to try today. Find as many ways as you can to give to others. Give money where appropriate, such as an extra big tip to the server at lunch, or a donation to a worthy charity.

Give to others in as many ways as possible. Give your time to help someone. Give your attention to someone who needs to be heard. Give your forgiveness, your gentleness, your peace, and your joy. Give a helping hand in as many ways, to as many people, as possible.

Abundance is a state of mind within you. If you just look at lack, the lack increases in life. See what you have, and then abundance increases.

—SRI SRI RAVI SHANKAR

THE ABILITY TO SEE
ABUNDANCE EVERYWHERE
MAKES YOU ABUNDANT

I went to a workshop a few years ago, and the teacher told us something that had a big impact on me. She said that no matter what happens to you, call it good.

Our knee-jerk reaction is to categorize experiences as positive or negative. But this teacher was showing us that by holding off our gut reactions, we allow ourselves to choose to see the best in every situation. In doing so, we open ourselves up to the best life has to offer. That's abundance.

Try This—Use What You Have Been Saving

A number of years ago, I bought a small box of very expensive candles (one box was all I could afford). The candles were exquisite, and came with beautiful glass holders. I put them in a drawer to keep them safe and protected.

Years went by, and every time I saw the candles, I always thought I was waiting for the "perfect" moment to light them. And then one day it occurred to me—what was I waiting for? Right now is the perfect moment. What are you holding onto, waiting for the "perfect moment"? Use it now!

Like the air you breathe,
abundance in all things is
available to you. Your life will
simply be as good as you
allow it to be.

—**ABRAHAM-HICKS**

THE ABUNDANCE OF NATURE

If you go for a walk, you will see the abundance of nature. Everywhere you look, you will see the evidence of how nature grows and expands.

How many grains of sand are there on a beach? How many blades of grass in that field? Even if you see an area filled with cement, gravel, and trash, you will see little plants sprouting up in the cracks. We are surrounded by abundance everywhere.

Try This—Tend Your Own Garden

Are your finances in good shape? Are your bills and assets all organized? Are you up to date on your accounts? If not, take this time to get everything in order. If you are a good steward with the money you have now, you'll be a good steward of the money you will receive in the future.

EBB AND FLOW

Have you heard about ebb and flow? If you watch nature, you will see that nothing is always in "flow." The tide goes in and out. Plants come and go. The day turns into night. Ebb and flow are natural in the scheme of life.

If you are experiencing an ebb in any area of your life, hold on, because the flow is coming. Flow always follows an ebb. We don't always know why, but the truth is that we need both.

Try This—Do Your Best Today

One of my friends told me that she wanted a promotion. A little while later she told me that she leaves at exactly 5 P.M., because she "isn't paid enough already," so why should she have to work any harder?

I suggested that instead of doing "just enough" at her job, she should try giving her absolute best every day and see if that made a difference in how she was perceived. She tried it, and was given a promotion just a few months later.

When we do our absolute best, we tend to experience more of what life has to give us. If we do "just enough," we'll always be lacking.

WHAT IS YOUR STORY: ABUNDANT OR LACK?

We often create limiting narratives about ourselves. A friend often tells me, "I only buy things on sale, because I just can't afford things that are full price. It would kill me to pay full price for anything." Another friend says, "I don't know why I'm always broke. I'm a good person, but I can't seem to catch a break." Still another says, "I wasn't born with a silver spoon in my mouth—everything is hard for me."

The story you tell yourself and others ends up becoming the truth about who you are. You can change the story you tell anytime and create a better outcome.

Make your life a masterpiece;
imagine no limitations on what
you can be, have, or do.

—**BRIAN TRACY**

Try This—Make It Fun

Striving and pushing for "more" can be exhausting. Constantly thinking that we have to do more, be more, have more can bring stress and depression. Why not try to turn things around and make them lighter . . . even fun?

When I was heavily in debt, everything felt difficult, and I felt like life was pressing in on me. I decided to find as many fun ways to help with my debt as I could.

I went to every free museum day around, I organized potlucks instead of going to restaurants, I participated in book swaps with my friends. Those, and dozens of other things I did, made getting out of debt less wearisome, and often fun.

5 WAYS TO KNOW YOU ARE MORE ABUNDANT

You smile and laugh throughout each day.

You find yourself grateful for what you have.

You are able to happily give to others in many ways.

You don't waste time on drama; you spend more time pursuing passions.

You choose to spend money on what makes you truly happy.

BE THE HERO IN YOUR ABUNDANCE STORY

Instead of waiting for a fairy godmother to come along and give you a castle, or waiting for a one-in-a-million lottery win, why not create your own magic and become your own hero?

You are your own strongest advocate. If you don't believe that, or feel that, then now is the time to start. Look in a mirror and tell yourself that *you* are the person you've been waiting for, that you are a person who can lift yourself up and create an abundant life.

Try This—Educate Yourself About Money and Investing

One of my friends recently got out of debt, and wanted to grow her wealth now that she had a little money each month to invest. The trouble was, she said, "I don't know anything about that stuff!"

She began by buying a book on the basics of investing and watching videos online, and slowly educated herself. She learned a great deal, and said she wished she had begun learning about money and investing years earlier. Start with a ten-minute video online, or a simple book on investing, and begin to increase your financial literacy.

ULTIMATE ABUNDANCE

Life can sometimes feel like the carnival whack-a-mole game. Just when you feel you have one area of your life in the flow of abundance, another area pops up with a problem. And once you've gotten that problem sorted out, yet another crops up.

It's hard to get everything flowing at the same time, in the same direction. And guess what?

That's not even really the goal. Ultimate abundance is when all of life happens, anything and everything, and you wouldn't change a thing.

Be content with what you
have, rejoice in the way things
are. When you realize there
is nothing lacking, the whole
world belongs to you.

—LAO-TZU

Bite-size guides to set you on the path to fulfillment—now!

ABUNDANCE
NOW

60 WAYS TO EXPERIENCE
TRUE ABUNDANCE

JESSE SANDS

HAPPINESS
NOW

60 WAYS TO EXPERIENCE
GENUINE HAPPINESS

JESSE SANDS

MINDFULNESS
NOW

60 WAYS TO EXPERIENCE
EFFORTLESS MINDFULNESS

JESSE SANDS

SIMPLICITY
NOW

60 WAYS TO EXPERIENCE
JOYFUL SIMPLICITY

JESSE SANDS

READ ALL OF THE NOW SERIES

Available Wherever Books Are Sold

ST. MARTIN'S
ESSENTIALS